Healthy Eating and Exercise

By

ANNE DAVIES and KERRY HUMES, M.D.

COPYRIGHT © 2008 Mark Twain Media, Inc.

ISBN 978-1-58037-449-1

Printing No. CD-404090

Mark Twain Media, Inc., Publishers
Distributed by Carson-Dellosa Publishing Company, Inc.

Table of Contents

Introduction

Healthy Eating and Exercise is an exciting new text designed to get students interested in taking charge of their diet and well-being. With soaring obesity rates among children and adults in the United States, it is important to give students the tools to make healthy choices. Whether it is choosing milk over soda in the school cafeteria, or taking the dog for a walk instead of playing a video game, this text helps students realize that the small things can add up to huge health benefits.

This book is organized into chapters that focus on the new food pyramid; breakfast, whole grains, and food labels; exercising; fruits and vegetables, sugar and caffeine; fats; protein; and food allergies, food-borne illnesses, and organic options. Each chapter begins with Teacher Notes, which offer suggestions for extending the lesson and answers to certain activities.

Some activities have an answer key designed to be copied and passed out to students to help them get the most out of the lesson. Other activities prompt critical thinking about such complex health issues as banning trans fats, buying organic foods, and decoding food labels. There are a variety of fun games, from Exercise Bingo to Who Wants to Be a Healthy-ionaire?, to engage students while reinforcing healthy choices.

By focusing on healthy choices, this text gives students the tools to become healthy adults without being preachy or overbearing. So have some fun with your students while building important health skills!

The New Food Pyramid

Teacher Notes:

The activities on the following pages introduce students to the new food pyramid, get them thinking positively about eating from all the sections of the pyramid, and help them set healthy eating and activity goals for themselves.

- You can extend the **Food Pyramid Favorites** activity by making a poster for your class with a combination of the students' different favorite foods. Draw an empty pyramid on a large sheet of paper, and then have the students draw or cut out pictures from grocery store advertisement sheets of their favorite foods and glue them on to the poster. Seeing different favorites may help students think about and try new foods in the different categories. You can also use the poster to discuss the idea of healthier foods within each category (whole grain bread vs. white bread; milk vs. ice cream, etc.).

- If you have easy access to multiple computers, you can have students put their own age/height/weight/activity level into the "MyPyramid Plan" calculator at the USDA website (www.mypyramid.gov) for individual daily calorie and serving recommendations. Alternatively, you can use the information below to give them some averages to chose from in completing the **How Did You Do Yesterday?** activity. You can use this page for a single day, or you can extend the activity by copying the sheet and making a booklet for each student to use for a week, a month, or more, depending on the time you and your students have for this activity.

> This 2,200 calorie food pattern is based on average needs for a 12-year-old male, of average height and weight, who is physically active 30 to 60 minutes a day.
>
> **Grains:** 7 ounces   **Fruit:** 2 cups   **Vegetables:** 3 cups
> **Milk:** 3 cups   **Meat & Beans:** 6 ounces
> **Oils:** aim for 6 teaspoons a day   **Extra Calories:** aim for 290 a day

> This 2,000 calorie food pattern is based on average needs for a 12-year-old female, of average height and weight, who is physically active 30 to 60 minutes a day.
>
> **Grains:** 6 ounces   **Fruit:** 2 cups   **Vegetables:** $2\frac{1}{2}$ cups
> **Milk:** 3 cups   **Meat & Beans:** $5\frac{1}{2}$ ounces
> **Oils:** aim for 6 teaspoons a day   **Extra Calories:** aim for 265 a day

- For **Food Group Bingo**, each student will need a single copy of one of the two bingo boards. Students should circulate around the class and find classmates who fit the different squares. A good rule is that you can only put a given classmate's initials on one box of the board, even if they can answer yes to several. This keeps everyone circulating and talking to all their classmates.

Name: _____   Date: _____

Food Pyramid Favorites

Where do your favorite foods fit in the food pyramid? Try to think of at least four favorites for each category. Remember, some prepared foods, like pizza, might fit into several different categories at the same time (grains for the crust, vegetables for the sauce and any veggie toppings, dairy for the cheese).

Grains	Vegetables	Fruits	Fats	Milk	Meat & Beans
_____	_____	_____	_____	_____	_____
_____	_____	_____	_____	_____	_____
_____	_____	_____	_____	_____	_____
_____	_____	_____	_____	_____	_____

Favorite forms of exercise:

1. _____
2. _____
3. _____
4. _____

Name: _____ Date: _____

How Did You Do Yesterday?

Did you eat your recommended number of servings from each of the food groups yesterday? Use this form to record what you ate yesterday, the recommended number of servings for each group, and your physical activities. Were you close? Give yourself a grade and a goal!

Grains	Veggies	Fruits	Milk	Meat & Beans	Fats, Oils, & Extras	Physical Activity
I Need:	I Need:	I Need:	I Need:	I Need:	I Need:	I Need:
I Ate:	I Ate:	I Ate:	I Ate:	I Ate:	I Ate:	I Did:

I would give myself a _____ for healthy activity and eating yesterday.

My goal for tomorrow is _____.

Name: _____ Date: _____

Food Group Bingo

Find a classmate who fits each box on your bingo board and write his or her initials in that box. When you have five in a row, you've won! You can also try to "black out" your board by finding someone to fit each box.

Food Bingo Card 1

Ate an orange fruit or veggie today	Ate whole wheat yesterday or today	Has had at least 1 serving of milk today	Has eaten protein today	Ate a green veggie yesterday
Ate a white veggie yesterday or today	Ate a blue fruit yesterday or today	Likes oatmeal or a cold oat cereal	Ate corn today	Likes raisins
Likes sweet potatoes	Likes melon	Has eaten tofu	Likes carrots	Ate rice today or yesterday
Ate a red fruit today or yesterday	Ate breakfast today	Ate lettuce yesterday or today	Ate a banana this week	Ate cheese today
Ate nuts this week	Likes tomatoes	Ate a whole grain today or yesterday	Likes mango, kiwi, or pomegranate	Likes fish

Name: _____ Date: _____

Food Group Bingo

Find a classmate who fits each box on your bingo board and write his or her initials in that box. When you have five in a row, you've won! You can also try to "black out" your board by finding someone to fit each box.

Food Bingo Card 2

Ate dried fruit this week	Ate an orange fruit or veggie yesterday	Had 3 servings of dairy yesterday	Ate peas or beans in the last 3 days	Ate corn yesterday or today
Likes tomatoes	Ate cheese yesterday or today	Has eaten protein today	Ate pork yesterday or today	Ate a green veggie today
Ate a blue fruit today	Ate a red fruit today or yesterday	Ate a white veggie this week	Likes brown rice	Likes spinach
Likes yogurt	Ate a whole grain today	Ate breakfast today	Likes rye bread	Likes cantaloupe or watermelon
Ate beans yesterday or today	Likes eggplant	Has eaten a sweet potato this week	Ate rice yesterday or today	Likes broccoli

Breakfast, Whole Grains, & Decoding Labels

Teacher Notes:

- Eating a healthy breakfast strongly correlates to overall healthy eating, as well as to good school performance. The activities on the following pages are designed to give students information about the importance of breakfast, to introduce the importance of whole grains, and to give them some basic information about reading nutritional labels. The answer sheet for **What's Your Breakfast IQ?** is meant to be given to each student to read, since it includes additional health information.

- If you have parents who can bring in different fruits and a few blenders, consider having your students try out and then taste test each other's smoothies when they do the **Invent Your Ideal Smoothie!** activity.

- For **Please Pass the Cereal**, you will need at least two boxes of cereal, several bowls, and a measuring cup. For the first cereal, try to have a relatively healthy whole grain cereal like Cheerios™ or Wheaties™. For the second cereal, use a cereal marketed to kids specifically, such as Frosted Flakes™ or Apple Jacks™. Ask several students to come up and pour what they think is a reasonable serving of cereal. Every student should select the bowl that they think is the amount they would typically eat. Measure the amount of cereal each student pours and write the volume on that bowl's label. Then measure out the recommended serving size for each kind of cereal. This activity highlights the fact that the serving size listed doesn't usually match what most of us eat at one sitting. After you've compared the official serving size to what the students would normally eat, identify the nutrition label information from the box. Students should compare the nutrition information, especially total sugars, fats, and calories, for the recommended serving size and the amount they would actually eat. This also reinforces math skills in everyday life. To continue the lesson, students can fill in the information for a favorite cereal of their own, using labels from home or from the Internet.

- You can use the **Blind Taste Test Tasting Notes** form for a blind taste test of four different kinds of bread or toast. You can also use the form to compare other foods. Be sure to include one choice that uses processed white flour and three other choices that include varying amounts of whole grains.

- For the **Hide and Go Seek** activity, you can bring in food packages for students to use, have them bring them in from home, or get information from the websites of major food companies.

- For **Designer Food Labels**, use the **Pumpkin Oatmeal Muffin Recipe** on page 15 for the nutritional information.

- For the **Too Much, Too Little, or Just Right?** activity, students can work in small groups. Each group will need a class list so they can keep track of who they have surveyed.

Breakfast, Whole Grains, & Decoding Labels (cont.)

Web Resources:

For the Cheerios™ portion size and nutritional information activity on page 13, visit:
http://www.generalmills.com/corporate/brands/brand.aspx?catID=53

For Frosted Flakes™ visit:
http://www2.kelloggs.com/Product/ProductDetail.aspx?product=450.

The General Mills and Kelloggs sites have the nutritional labels for many other cereals as well. Most major food producers now have this information on their websites, as do most well-known fast-food chains.

The FDA site with information on reading labels is:
http://www.cfsan.fda.gov/~dms/foodlab.html

For more information about whole grains, visit:
http://www.wholegrainscouncil.org

At http://www.cfsan.fda.gov/~dms/spotov.html your students can watch a public service ad that ran on the Cartoon Network to get kids focused on nutritional labels. Have your students watch and discuss if the ad is effective or not and why.

For nutritional information on many common fruits, visit:
http://www.dole5aday.com/Kids/K_Index.jsp

Name: _____ Date: _____

What's Your Breakfast IQ?

Circle the correct answer.

1. The first breakfast cereal served in colonial America was:

    a. toasted wheat with maple syrup and cream   b. popped corn with sugar and cream
    c. toasted oats served with honey and cream   d. puffed rice with honey and sugar

2. People who eat breakfast are _____ less likely to be obese than those who don't.

    a. 10–20%   b. 30–50%   c. 60–70%

3. Fresh fruit, yogurt, and khichri (a mixture of rice, lentils, and spices) are common breakfast foods in this country.

    a. China   b. England   c. France   d. India

4. Approximately _____ of Americans eat cereal for breakfast.

    a. 25%   b. 50%   c. 75%   d. 100%

5. Toast topped with spaghetti or baked beans and bacon is a popular breakfast in this country.

    a. France   b. Australia   c. Japan   d. Lebanon

6. People who eat a healthy breakfast are more likely to:

    a. do well in school.   b. have more strength and endurance.
    c. control their weight.   d. concentrate well in the morning.
    e. all of the above.

7. Circle the cereals listed below that you think use whole grains.

    a. Cinnamon Toast Crunch™   b. Fruit Loops™   c. Wheaties™
    d. Honey Bunches of Oats™   e. Frosted Flakes™   f. Cheerios™
    g. Mini Swirlz Cinnamon Buns™   h. Chex™   i. Life™

8. Circle the foods that would add protein to your breakfast:

    a. yogurt   b. tea   c. eggs   d. toast
    e. cheese   h. coffee   i. orange juice j. pancakes

What's Your Breakfast IQ?
Answers

Give yourself one point for each correct answer.

1. *b.* The first breakfast cereal served in colonial America was popped corn with sugar and cream. Popular cereals today commonly use corn, wheat, oats, and rice. Most have some sugar added, but some have a great deal more sugar added. A healthy choice is a cereal where most of the carbohydrates are from the grains, not the sugars.

2. *b.* People who eat breakfast are 30–50% less likely to be obese than those who don't.

3. *d.* Fresh fruit, yogurt, and khichri are common breakfast foods in India. This is a well-balanced breakfast supplying fruit, dairy, grains, and protein.

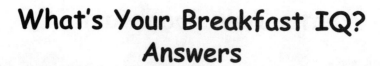

4. *b.* Approximately 50% of Americans eat cereal for breakfast. Some cereals make a very healthy whole-grain breakfast, with most of the calories coming from the whole grains. Others have a huge amount of added sugar. These are not as healthy.

5. *b.* Toast topped with spaghetti or baked beans and bacon is a popular breakfast in Australia.

6. *e.* People who eat a healthy breakfast are more likely to do and be all of these things! Give yourself 5 points if you answered "all of the above;" otherwise, give yourself 1 point for each of the things you circled.

7. *a., c., d., f., h., i.* Cinnamon Toast Crunch™, Wheaties™, Honey Bunches of Oats™, Cheerios™, Chex™ and Life™ are all made with whole grains. Whole grain cereals are a better choice than cereals without whole grain, but you still need to think about added sugar. For example, Honey Nut Cheerios™ has much more added sugar than plain Cheerios™. Give yourself 1 point for each whole grain cereal you correctly identified (subtract 1 point for any non-whole grain cereal you circled).

8. *a., c., e.* Yogurt, eggs, and cheese would add protein to your breakfast. Give yourself 1 point for each protein food you correctly identified (subtract 1 point for any non-protein food you circled).

Scoring:
17–19: You're ready for a Ph.D. Great job!
10–17: You've been paying attention. Good work!
0–10: You're on your way, but keep studying. Your body will thank you!

Name: _____ Date: _____

Fruit Smoothies

Don't like cereal? Don't like eggs and toast? Don't worry! Get out your favorite fruits, some juice or yogurt, and make yourself a fruit smoothie for a quick and delicious alternative breakfast! It's almost like having a milk shake for breakfast!

A 'Berry' Good Breakfast

An all-fruit classic with lots of vitamin C!

Ingredients
1 banana

$1\frac{1}{2}$ cups of your favorite frozen berries (you can use all one type of berries or a combination)

1 cup of orange or pineapple juice

Directions
Cut the banana into 3 or 4 pieces. Put all the ingredients in a blender and blend until smooth. Enjoy!

A Mango Lassi

This smoothie includes dairy as well as fruit.

Ingredients

1 mango
1 cup of low fat yogurt
2 ice cubes

Directions

Cut the mango into quarters. Put all the ingredients in a blender and blend until smooth. Freezing the yogurt ahead of time makes the smoothie colder. If you prefer a sweeter smoothie, add a teaspoon of honey. Enjoy!

Nutritional Information:

1 banana:
3 grams of fiber
45 IU vitamin A
11 mg vitamin C
467 mg potassium

1 mango:
3 grams of fiber
8,060 IU vitamin A
57 mg vitamin C
323 mg potassium

$\frac{1}{2}$ cup blackberries:
7 grams of fiber
237 IU vitamin A
30 mg vitamin C
282 mg potassium

$\frac{1}{2}$ cup raspberries:
4 grams of fiber
20 IU vitamin A
16 mg vitamin C
93 mg potassium

$\frac{1}{2}$ cup blueberries:
1.7 grams of fiber
39 IU vitamin A
7 mg vitamin C
56 mg potassium

$\frac{1}{2}$ cup strawberries:
3 grams of fiber
39 IU vitamin A
82 mg vitamin C
239 mg potassium

Name: _____ Date: _____

Invent Your Ideal Smoothie!

You can use any combination of fruits you like, along with juice, yogurt, or ice, to make a smoothie. If you like a lighter taste, add ice cubes. For a colder taste sensation, use frozen fruit, or freeze an ice cube tray with juice. With taste and nutrition in mind, design your own ideal smoothie and write the recipe below.

Ingredients: _____

_____

_____

_____

_____

Directions: _____

_____

_____

_____

_____

_____

_____

_____

Nutrition: _____

_____

_____

_____

_____

1 kiwi:
3.1 grams of fiber
159 IU vitamin A
68 mg vitamin C
302 mg potassium

1 apple:
3.3 grams of fiber
75 IU vitamin A
6 mg vitamin C
148 mg potassium

1 peach:
1.5 grams of fiber
319 IU vitamin A
7 mg vitamin C
189 mg potassium

1 pear:
5.1 grams of fiber
38 IU vitamin A
7 mg vitamin C
198 mg potassium

$\frac{1}{2}$ cup cantaloupe:
0.7 grams of fiber
2,706 IU vitamin A
30 mg vitamin C
214 mg potassium

Name: _____ Date: _____

Please Pass the Cereal

What's a serving size? Compare the recommended serving size with what you would normally eat for two different cereals. How close are you?

Cereal #1 _____

Nutrition Information for the recommended serving size:

Amount: _____
Calories: _____
Total Fat: _____
Carbohydrates: _____
Dietary Fiber: _____
Protein: _____
Vitamin A: _____
Vitamin C: _____
Calcium: _____
Iron: _____
Vitamin D: _____

Nutrition Information for the serving size you chose:

Amount: _____
Calories: _____
Total Fat: _____
Carbohydrates: _____
Dietary Fiber: _____
Protein: _____
Vitamin A: _____
Vitamin C: _____
Calcium: _____
Iron: _____
Vitamin D: _____

Cereal #2 _____

Nutrition Information for the recommended serving size:

Amount: _____
Calories: _____
Total Fat: _____
Carbohydrates: _____
Dietary Fiber: _____
Protein: _____
Vitamin A: _____
Vitamin C: _____
Calcium: _____
Iron: _____
Vitamin D: _____

Nutrition Information for the serving size you chose:

Amount: _____
Calories: _____
Total Fat: _____
Carbohydrates: _____
Dietary Fiber: _____
Protein: _____
Vitamin A: _____
Vitamin C: _____
Calcium: _____
Iron: _____
Vitamin D: _____

Name: _____ Date: _____

Blind Taste Test Tasting Notes

What makes something taste good? Taste test four different kinds of bread (or other food). After tasting each sample, make notes in the box about what you thought of it and why you did or did not like it. Then give each sample a rating of one to three stars, with three stars being the best.

Sample #1
Notes: ☆☆☆

Sample #2
Notes: ☆☆☆

Sample #3
Notes: ☆☆☆

Sample #4
Notes: ☆☆☆

My favorite for taste was _____.

Considering taste *and* health, I'd pick _____.

The Whole Story:

All grains are seeds. If something is made with a whole grain, that means all three parts of the grain kernel—the bran, the germ, and the endosperm—are used. The **bran** is the outer layer that protects the seed. It has fiber, minerals like iron and potassium, and B vitamins. The **germ** is the part of the seed that would grow into a new plant if we didn't harvest and eat it. It also has B vitamins, some minerals, vitamin E, and protein. The inside of the kernel is the part that would feed a baby plant, and it is called the **endosperm.** It has starchy carbohydrates and some protein, but not as many vitamins and minerals as the two other parts. White, or refined, flour only uses the endosperm part of the wheat kernel. Whole grains use the entire seed—the bran, the germ, and the endosperm.

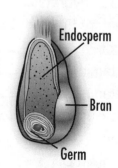

Pumpkin Oatmeal Muffins

These tasty muffins are made with whole grain oatmeal and delicious pumpkin as well!

Dry Ingredients:

1 $\frac{1}{4}$ cup quick oats, uncooked

1 $\frac{1}{4}$ cup unbleached all-purpose flour

$\frac{1}{2}$ cup firmly packed brown sugar

1 tablespoon baking powder

$\frac{1}{2}$ teaspoon baking soda

$\frac{1}{2}$ teaspoon salt

1 $\frac{1}{2}$ teaspoons ground ginger

1 $\frac{1}{2}$ teaspoons ground cinnamon

$\frac{1}{4}$ teaspoon ground cloves

1 tablespoon of oats (for topping)

2 teaspoons brown sugar (for topping)

Wet Ingredients:

1 cup canned pure pumpkin puree

$\frac{3}{4}$ cup milk

$\frac{1}{3}$ cup vegetable oil

1 egg

Directions:
Preheat the oven to 400°F. Line twelve medium muffin cups with paper baking cups or spray with cooking spray.

Use a whisk to mix the oats, flour, sugar, baking powder, baking soda, salt, ginger, cinnamon and cloves together in a large bowl.

In a medium bowl, combine the pumpkin, milk, oil, and egg. Blend well.

Add the wet ingredients to the dry ingredients all at once; stir just until dry ingredients are moistened. Do not overmix.

Fill the muffin cups about two-thirds full of batter. Sprinkle the tops of each with a pinch of brown sugar and a pinch of oats.

Bake 22 to 25 minutes, or until tops are browned. Cool muffins in pan for 5 minutes. Serve and enjoy!

Hide and Go Seek
or How to Read Food Labels

The label on a food package tells you what's in that food, right? Well, kind of. Food manufacturers have to list the ingredients, but they don't have to make it easy to understand. Packaging can make a product seem healthier than it is, unless you know the tricks. Here are some rules about food labels and some tricks manufacturers can use to get around those rules.

Rule 1: Food labels must list ingredients in order from highest percentage to lowest percentage. If *water* is the first ingredient listed on a juice cocktail bottle, and *apple juice* is third, that means that there is more water than real juice in the cocktail.

Trick: Manufactures may use two or three different sweeteners so sugar doesn't have to be listed first. Learn the different types of sweeteners to avoid falling for this trick.

Different names for sweeteners:
sucrose, glucose, dextrose, corn syrup, fructose, fruit juice concentrate, honey, molasses

Different names for salt:
sodium chloride, monosodium glutamate

Rule 2: In order to write **Whole Grain** on the package, the food must be made of whole grains.

Trick: There are no requirements for the amount of whole grains a product must have to be labeled **whole grain**. Manufacturers add just a little whole grain, while using mainly processed grains, so they can say **Whole Grain** on the label. Some manufactures use food coloring to make their product look like it has more whole grains than it really does. To avoid this, look for the label "Diets rich in whole grain foods and other plant foods and low in total fat, saturated fat, and cholesterol may reduce the risk of heart disease and some cancers." A product has to have at least 51% whole grain ingredients by weight and also be low in fat and a good source of fiber to have this label.

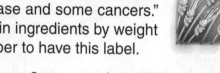

Rule 3: To claim that something is **Low Fat**, it has to have 3 grams or less of fat per serving. Only 30% of the total calories can be from fat.

Trick: If something is labeled **Reduced Fat**, there only has to be 25% less fat in that product than in the product it is being compared to. Manufacturers also may reduce the fat in a food, but increase the sugar in a product. The food may taste good, but it still may not be all that healthy. Be sure to read the label to find out what's really in a product.

Rule 4: Products labeled **All Natural** or **Organic** are healthy.

Trick: These are not labels with clear meanings. Sometimes, as with whole grains, when something has **Organic** on the package, that means that a small part is organic, but the rest isn't. **All Natural** sounds healthy, but just because something sounds healthy, doesn't mean it is. Sugar is natural, but in large quantities, it isn't good for you. And what about something like high fructose corn syrup? It's made from corn, which is natural, but it is highly processed. Reading the fine print on a label is the only way to be sure.

16

Name: _____ Date: _____

Hide and Go Seek
or How to Read Food Labels (cont.)

Where's the line between truthy and tricky? You decide. Pick one food label and give it a grade for honesty.

I evaluated the label on _____

I think it (was / was not) trying to hide information.

Easy-to-understand ingredients: _____

_____

_____

Not-so-easy-to-understand ingredients: _____

_____

_____

This is what I noticed most about the label: _____

_____

_____

_____

Are there any ways this label could be more honest? _____

_____

_____

Overall, I would give this food label
(The more stars, the better.)  for honesty.

Name: _____ Date: _____

Designer Food Labels

Congratulations! You and a friend have just decided to start your own company selling Pumpkin Oatmeal Muffins. You have perfected the recipe. Now all you need to do is design your label. You plan to make six oversized muffins from each batch of the Pumpkin Oatmeal Muffin recipe on page 15 and sell them as one package. Use the form below to create a label that you think will help sell your muffins, that is honest, and that includes a list of ingredients.

Remember that in a recipe, ingredients are usually listed in the order used, but on a food label, you need to list them in order of highest percentage of finished product to lowest percentage of finished product.

Name: _____ Date: _____

Too Much, Too Little, or Just Right?

Survey your classmates to find out how many people ate less than, more than, or the recommended daily serving amount yesterday of one of the Food Pyramid categories. You won't keep track of individual names, just the numbers for the class as a whole.

Pick one of the categories from the Food Pyramid:
grains; vegetables; fruits; oils; milk; meat & beans _____

What is the recommended daily serving suggestion for your category? _____

Before you start your survey, make a prediction. What percentage of the class do you think will have eaten:

    Less Than Recommended: _____

    Just What's Recommended: _____

    More Than Recommended: _____

Place one tally mark per student in the appropriate column.

Less	Just What's Recommended	More

Now use the pie chart to graph your findings:

Exercise: Calories In, Calories Out

Teacher Notes:

Students can be easily confused by all the different messages about exercise and calories in our culture. This unit focuses on having fun with exercise, maintaining balance, and being aware that how we choose to spend our day has a lasting impact on our bodies.

- For **You Won!,** you may want to establish rules, such as students can't use an activity more than once in a week, or they have to have at least three new activities each week. This will push them to imagine trying new kinds of exercise.

- Answer key for **What's Your Guess:** (All answers are approximate calories per hour)

1. 472	2. 177	3. 413	4. 738	5. 177	6. 207
7. 207	8. 236	9. 590	10. 472	11. 649	12. 885
13. 295	14. 413	15. 590	16. 413	17. 177	18. 295
19. 236	20. 61				

- **Exercise Bingo** works just like the **Food Groups Bingo** on pages 5 and 6.

- The **Balance the Scale** Food and Exercise Cards can be used in a number of different ways:
  1. Students can pick a food they like to eat and match it with an exercise that roughly balances it.
  2. Students can think about and plan a day of exercise, rest, and eating.
  3. Both sets of cards can be used to help with other activities throughout the book, including **Menus for a Day** on page 27.
  4. On the page following the **Exercise Cards**, there is a blank grid for students to use to create their own food or exercise cards.

- Having students create their own cards is especially important for additional foods your students like to eat. Many activities, like **Menus for a Day,** will be most meaningful if students use foods they eat. For calorie information, consider either printing out nutritional information from food manufacturers' websites or asking your students to bring in clean, empty food packaging from home.

Web Resources:

A wonderful resource for encouraging physical fitness is the President's Physical Fitness Challenge: www.presidentschallenge.org

Consider whether your class might take on encouraging your school to be a model school in the program as a service project.

Name: _____ Date: _____

*Baseball * Soccer * Yoga * Basketball * Biking * Golf * Hip-Hop Dancing * Gymnastics * Rock Climbing * Skateboarding * Football * Sea kayaking * White water kay*

You Won!

Congratulations! You just won a month-long trip to a famous exercise-oriented resort. They have every kind of exercise equipment you can imagine and people there to teach you any new sport you'd like to try. What would you like to do each day? Fill in each day in the month with something you'd like to try. You can find some ideas in the border on this page, or you can think up some of your own.

Bonus: For one day only, you get to work with the coach of your dreams—you can pick any professional (or nonprofessional) athlete, coach, dancer, yoga teacher, or martial artist, and they'll work with you that day!

Monday	Tuesday	Wednesday	Thursday	Friday	Saturday	Sunday

My dream coach: _____

21

Name: _____ Date: _____

What's Your Guess?

Exercise is an essential part of staying healthy. Exercise is a lot like school. The more you put into it, the more your heart, muscles, and bones get out of it. When it comes to burning calories, remember, the more you weigh, the more calories you burn. Did you know it takes 3,500 calories to lose (or gain!) one pound?

Below are different types of exercise and activities. Working with a partner, estimate how many calories you think a 130-pound person would burn if he or she did each activity for one hour.

Example: Swimming laps burns 470 calories in an hour.

1. Playing in a basketball game: _____
2. Bicycling (light effort): _____
3. Bicycling (moderate effort): _____
4. Bicycling (vigorous/racing): _____
5. Bowling: _____
6. Cleaning house: _____
7. Ultimate frisbee: _____
8. Raking the lawn: _____
9. Jumping rope: _____
10. Running a 12-minute mile: _____
11. Running a 9-minute mile: _____
12. Running a 6-minute mile: _____
13. Skateboarding: _____
14. Sledding: _____
15. Competitive soccer: _____
16. Casual soccer: _____
17. Surfing: _____
18. Whitewater rafting or kayaking: _____
19. Horseback riding: _____
20. Sleeping: _____

Name: _____ Date: _____

Exercise Bingo

Find a classmate to fit each box on your bingo board and write his or her initials in that box. When you have 5 in a row, you've won! You can also try to "black out" your board by finding someone to fit each box.

Has used a stairmaster	Can do double-dutch jump rope	Would like to try a bicycle built for two	Can do 30 sit ups	Likes playing football
Plays basketball	Can juggle 3 balls at a time	Knows the rules of dodgeball	Likes playing soccer	Has gotten a strike while bowling
Likes bike riding	Could teach someone how to hit a baseball	Can jump rope backwards	Likes running	Likes dancing
Likes sledding	Knows how to serve in volleyball	Has gone skiing	Has played on a soccer team	Could teach someone how to skateboard
Does martial arts	Likes swimming	Has tried ice skating	Can do 40 jumping jacks	Knows how to hula hoop

Name: _____ Date: _____

Balance the Scale
Food Cards

1 Slice Pizza Hut™ cheese pizza: 220 calories	Four Oreos™: 100 calories	11 mini Nilla Wafers™: 150 calories	1 apple: 80 calories	1 Bowl of Life™ cereal w/skim milk: 160 calories
1 Kudos™ bar: 100 calories	1 cup of 1% chocolate milk: 170 calories	1 container of strawberry yogurt: 170 calories	1 cheese square: 80 calories	8 oz. glass of orange juice: 110 calories
1 ice cream sandwich: 160 calories	1 grilled chicken sandwich: 340 calories	1 peanut butter and jelly sandwich: 400 calories	1 grilled chicken breast: 140 calories	1 piece of carrot cake: 480 calories
1 cup of watermelon: 25 calories	1 peach: 40 calories	1 bagel: 330 calories	1 Eggo™ waffle: 100 calories	1 soft pretzel: 225 calories
1 garlic bread stick: 150 calories	1 serving of pasta: 220 calories	1 piece of toast with butter: 100 calories	$\frac{1}{2}$ cup of ice cream: 170 calories	5 french toast sticks: 330 calories
1 Pop Tart™: 190 calories	7 Triscuit™ crackers: 120 calories	1 fat-free cheese slice: 30 calories	55 Goldfish™ pieces: 140 calories	1 mini box of raisins: 45 calories

Name: _____ Date: _____

Balance the Scale
Exercise Cards

Calories burned are per hour.

Backpacking: 207 calories	Basketball: 236 calories	Bicycling: 236 calories	Boxing: 250 calories	Canoeing: 125 calories
Circuit training: 236 calories	Construction work: 165 calories	Cooking: 75 calories	Dancing: 133 calories	Fishing: 100 calories
Farming: 225 calories	Playing catch: 70 calories	Football: 235 calories	Golf: 115 calories	Gymnastics: 120 calories
Hockey: 235 calories	Jogging: 205 calories	Kickball: 205 calories	Lacrosse: 235 calories	Marching band: 120 calories
Mowing the lawn: 160 calories	Playing an instrument: 75 calories	Walking rapidly: 190 calories	Racquetball: 205 calories	Sailing: 150 calories
Shoveling snow: 175 calories	Cross country skiing: 235 calories	Downhill skiing: 175 calories	Snowmobiling: 100 calories	Swimming laps: 470 calories

25

Name: _____ Date: _____

Balance the Scale
Additional Food/Exercise Cards

Name: _____ Date: _____

Menus for a Day

Design a delicious day of eating for someone who'd like to eat 1,800 calories.

Breakfast	Lunch	Dinner	Snacks

Design a delicious day of eating for someone who'd like to eat 2,000 calories.

Breakfast	Lunch	Dinner	Snacks

Design a delicious day of eating for someone who'd like to eat 2,200 calories.

Breakfast	Lunch	Dinner	Snacks

Name: _____ Date: _____

My Exercise Log

Cut out the tags below on the dotted lines, put them in order, and staple them together. Record the type of exercise you did and how long you did it for each day. Then rate your exercise. Was it a 1-star day, where you exercised some, but not a total of 60 minutes? Was it a 2-star day, where you exercised for a total of 60 minutes? Or was it a 3-star day, where you exercised more than 60 minutes or tried something new?

Monday

☆ ☆ ☆

Tuesday

☆ ☆ ☆

Wednesday

☆ ☆ ☆

Thursday

☆ ☆ ☆

Friday

☆ ☆ ☆

Saturday

☆ ☆ ☆

Sunday

☆ ☆ ☆

A Focus on Fruits & Vegetables, Sugar & Caffeine

Teacher Notes:

There are many choices we can make when choosing a meal, a beverage, or even a snack. It is important that students understand that these choices impact their health. The exercises below involve fruits and vegetables, which have huge benefits for our bodies, as well as sugar and caffeine, which can cause trouble when we don't consume them wisely.

- The **What Do You Know? What Do You Wonder?** page can be used as a pre-assessment to check students' levels of knowledge. It's meant to pique their interest and prompt questions.

- For **Eating Across the Rainbow**, students should be broken into groups of 3 or 4. Groups should prepare their answers separately, and then come together to compare and score answers. Have the class make a poster of their answers as they read through them. Possible answers include:
    Red: beets, red cabbage, cranberries, strawberries, pomegranates, rhubarb, cherries, red apples, or tomatoes.
    Yellow/Orange: apricots, butternut squash, carrots, grapefruit, lemons, oranges, papayas, or sweet potatoes.
    Green: asparagus, broccoli, cucumbers, kiwi, green beans, peas, lettuce, or spinach.
    Blue/Purple: blackberries, blueberries, eggplant, plums, prunes, figs, or raisins.
    White: potatoes, cauliflower, mushrooms, garlic, ginger, onions, turnips, or parsnips.

- Answers for **Have a Sip of Sugar**: In order from least to most sugar:
    soda water, Diet Coke™, Gatorade™, cranberry juice, Sprite™, Coke™, Pepsi™, root beer, orange juice, Mountain Dew™, Code Red™, and orange soda.

- The answer sheets for **What's Your Sugar IQ?** and **Caffeine 101** are designed to give students additional information about the topics addressed.

- The **Lemonade Taste Test and Analysis** will work best if you compare a powdered lemonade mix, a frozen lemonade mix, a fresh lemonade from the juice section of the grocery store, and homemade lemonade from fresh lemons. We've included a homemade lemonade recipe that has a good amount of vitamins and fiber. Adjust the sugar to taste.

- After students make their guesses for **Calculate the Caffeine**, discuss the average amounts. Students can graph the results on **A Caffeine Graph** for a visual reminder of the differences between these choices. Listed from most caffeine to least, with 12 oz. for all beverages: coffee: 250 mg; two NoDoz™ tablets: 200 mg; black tea: 70 mg; Mountain Dew™: 55 mg; coffee ice cream: 50 mg per cup; Diet Coke™: 45 mg; Pepsi™: 38 mg; Coke™: 34 mg; dark chocolate bar: 30 mg; brownie: 15 mg; hot chocolate: 14 mg; milk chocolate bar: 10 mg; 7-Up™: 0 mg.

Web Resources:

The American Institute for Cancer Research: www.aicr.org

The CDC's site for healthy eating: www.fruitsandveggiesmatter.gov

Name: _____ Date: _____

What Do You Know? What Do You Wonder?

What do you already know about vitamins and minerals in fruits and vegetables?

What do you wonder about vitamins and minerals in fruits and vegetables?

_____
_____
_____
_____
_____

Are vitamins from a pill the same as vitamins in a veggie?

_____
_____
_____
_____
_____

What happens if you eat more than the recommended daily allowance?

_____
_____
_____
_____

_____
_____
_____
_____
_____

Is more always better with minerals and vitamins?

_____
_____
_____
_____
_____

_____
_____

Do fruits and veggies of the same color have the same vitamins and minerals in them?

_____
_____

Name: _____ Date: _____

Eating Across the Rainbow

How many fruits and vegetables can you list for each color of the rainbow? Each team gets 1 point for each fruit or vegetable listed. If you list a fruit or vegetable that no other team does, your team gets 3 points!

Red

points: _____

Yellow & Orange

points: _____

Green

points: _____

Blue & Purple

points: _____

White

points: _____

Total points: _____

Building a Healthy Body

To keep your body healthy, you need many vitamins and minerals. Some of the most important ones are listed below, along with some of the foods that are among the best sources for those vitamins and minerals. Grains, especially whole grains, also supply vitamins. Many processed grain products are vitamin fortified, meaning they've had vitamins added back in. Most experts think getting vitamins directly from fruits, vegetables, and grains, rather than from fortified products or from vitamin pills, is best for your body.

Potassium builds muscles.

Get potassium from: avocados, bananas, kiwis, artichokes, lima beans, potatoes, sweet potatoes, peaches, bok choy, pears, celery, zucchini, peas, corn, spinach, squash, asparagus

Vitamin C and *vitamin E* keep skin smooth.

Get vitamin C from: kiwis, strawberries, oranges, broccoli, peppers, peas, grapefruit
Get vitamin E from: mango, kiwis, blackberries

Calcium and *vitamin D* make teeth and bones strong.

Get calcium from: artichokes, broccoli, peas, kiwis, oranges, blackberries, milk, yogurt, cheese
Get vitamin D from: mushrooms, sunshine (Most people only need about 10 minutes a day. Always wear sunscreen.)

Vitamin A strengthens hair and eyes.

Get vitamin A from: carrots, sweet potatoes, spinach, mangos, cantaloupe, tomatoes, lettuce, pumpkin, bok choy, red peppers, apricots, collard greens

Vitamin K helps blood clot.

Get vitamin K from: broccoli, kale, spinach

Folate helps women have healthy babies.

Get folate from: artichokes, asparagus, lima beans, avocados, kiwis, strawberries

Name: _____ Date: _____

How Many Times Can You Hit the Bell?

Are you building a healthy body for yourself? Using the information from the **Building a Healthy Body** sheet, count how many vitamin and mineral-rich foods you have eaten in the last three days. Color in the sections of each bell, up to four, for each serving of a vitamin or mineral you have had. Have you hit the bell for any?

Vitamin A

Vitamin D

Vitamin C

Vitamin E

Potassium

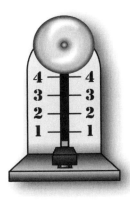

Calcium

Vitamin K

Folate

Name: _____ Date: _____

Desert Island Diet

The bad news: You are headed to a desert island for six months. The island has no fruits or vegetables growing on it; in fact, nothing edible grows there.

The good news: There are some nonedible trees that provide shade and wood for a fire, and there are plenty of fish you can catch for protein. You also get to have a magic suitcase with you. You can pack three fruits or vegetables, one kind of grain, and one kind of dairy into this suitcase. Each night, while you sleep, your supply of these foods will be replenished.

What foods would you want in your magical suitcase?

Fruits and Vegetables:

1. _____

2. _____

3. _____

Grain:

1. _____

Dairy

1. _____

Vitamins & minerals supplied by your food choices:

_____

_____

_____

_____

_____

_____

Name: _____ Date: _____

Have a Sip of Sugar

Below is a list of a dozen drinks. Work with a partner to put them in order from the least amount of sugar to the most. Check the nutrition labels or the Internet to find the sugar content.

orange juice	Coke™	Diet Coke™	Gatorade™
orange soda	root beer	cranberry juice	Pepsi™
Code Red™	Sprite™	Mountain Dew™	soda water

The least sugar

1. _____

2. _____

3. _____

4. _____

5. _____

6. _____

7. _____

8. _____

9. _____

10. _____

11. _____

12. _____

The most sugar

Drinking soft drinks has been linked to an increase in obesity, tooth decay, and weakened bones.

56% of 8-year-olds drink at least one soft drink per day.

15 billion gallons of soda were sold in the U.S. in 2000.

$\frac{1}{4}$ of all drinks consumed in the U.S. are soft drinks.

Name: _____ Date: _____

What's Your Sugar IQ?

Lots of processed foods include sweeteners, but it's not always easy to identify them from the label. Manufacturers may use ingredients with less familiar names, or they might use several different sweeteners. Test your sugar IQ by circling the correct choice below.

1. Which term is often used to describe sugar?

    a. Sucralose   b. Sucrose   c. Dextrose   d. Lactose   e. Maltose

2. Underline the natural sweeteners, circle the artificial sweeteners, and cross out the ingredients that are not sweeteners on this list:

Glycerol	Sucrose	Fructose	Honey	Neotame
Fruit juice concentrate		Malt extract	Aspartame	Riboflavin
Monosodium Glutamate		Maple Syrup	Corn syrup	Molasses

3. How many times sweeter is aspartame than sucrose?

    a. 200   b. 250   c. 180   d. 110   e. 75   f. 10

4. _____ of teenage boys drink three sodas per day.

    a. 10%   b. 25%   c. 33%   d. 50%   e. 75%

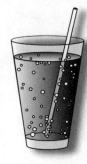

5. Honey can cause an allergic reaction in some people.   T   F

6. The advertising budget for soft drinks is approximately _____ per year.

    a. $2 million
    b. $5 million
    c. $25 million
    d. $2 billion
    e. $5 billion

What's Your Sugar IQ? Answers

Give yourself one point for each correct answer.

1. *b.* Sucrose.

2. Give yourself 1 point for each ingredient you correctly identified, but subtract one point for each ingredient you mislabeled.
Natural sweeteners: malt extract
fruit juice concentrate
glycerol
sucrose
fructose
honey
corn syrup
molasses
maple syrup
Artificial sweeteners: neotame
aspartame
Not sweeteners: riboflavin
monsodium glutamate

3. *c.* Aspartame is 180 times sweeter than sucrose.

4. *c.* 33% of teenage boys drink three sodas per day. This means they are either getting much more sugar than is recommended, or they are consuming a lot of artificial sweeteners, both of which can cause problems. In addition, drinking three sodas per day increases the risk of tooth decay, obesity, and weakened bones. What do you think a safe amount of soda is to drink? Bonus: Give yourself another point if you have not had a soda today.

5. *True*, honey can cause an allergic reaction.

6. *d.* The advertising budget for soft drinks is approximately $2 billion per year. Next time you think you want a soda, ask yourself, do I really *want* a soda, or has advertising just convinced me that I *should* want one?

Scoring:
17–19: You're ready for a Ph.D. Great job!
10–17: You've been paying attention. Good work!
0–10: You're on your way, but keep studying. Your body will thank you!

Name: _____ Date: _____

A Liquid Log

Did you know that water constitutes a great deal of our weight? Did you know that our bodies need water to maintain the integrity of cells, to help with digestion, and to regulate our body temperature? Water is essential to our existence! Most people need around 64 oz. of liquid per day to maintain a healthy level of water in our bodies (more if they are exercising heavily or live in a hot climate). The liquids you drink can be a source of nutrition or a source of "empty" calories. What do you drink each day? Keep track for a week.

Monday

Approximate total oz.: _____

Tuesday

Approximate total oz.: _____

Wednesday

Approximate total oz.: _____

Thursday

Approximate total oz.: _____

Friday

Approximate total oz.: _____

Saturday

Approximate total oz.: _____

Sunday

Approximate total oz.: _____

Homemade Lemonade

Makes 6 servings

Ingredients:
1 cup fresh squeezed lemon juice (about 5 to 6 lemons)
1 cup of sugar
1 cup of water
4 cups of cold water
ice

Cut the lemons in half, and squeeze them until you have one cup of lemon juice. Save at least one thin slice of lemon with which to garnish your lemonade. In a small pan, heat 1 cup of water with the sugar, stirring until the sugar completely dissolves. Then combine the sugar syrup with the fresh juice in a pitcher. Mix in the 4 cups of cold water and chill for 15 to 20 minutes. Serve over ice and garnish with a fresh lemon slice.

Note: Some people like tarter lemonade. You can try using $\frac{3}{4}$ cup of sugar.

Nutritional Information:

1 serving = $\frac{1}{6}$ of recipe, approximately 1 cup.
Calories: 151
Carbohydrates: 44.9 g
Sugar: 35.2 g
Fiber: 5.1 g
Vitamin C: 139% RDI
Calcium: 9% RDI
Iron: 8% RDI
Vitamin B6: 7% RDI
Thiamine: 5% RDI
Magnesium: 5% RDI
Folate: 4% RDI
Potassium: 4% RDI

Name: _____ Date: _____

Lemonade Taste Test and Analysis

What makes lemonade taste good? Taste test four different kinds of lemonade. After tasting each sample, make notes in the box about what you thought of it and why you did or did not like it. Then give each sample a rating of one to three stars, with three stars being the best.

Sample #1
Notes: ☆☆☆

Sample #2
Notes ☆☆☆

Sample #3
Notes ☆☆☆

Sample #4
Notes ☆☆☆

Sample #1 was _____
It used the following sweeteners: _____
Sample #2 was _____
It used the following sweeteners: _____
Sample #3 was _____
It used the following sweeteners: _____
Sample #4 was _____
It used the following sweeteners: _____

Sample # _____ has the highest sugar.
Sample # _____ has the most vitamins and minerals.
Sample # _____ has the most fiber.

I would recommend Sample # _____.

Fruit-Sweetened Treats

If you have a sweet tooth but want to be healthy, try one of these fruit-sweetened treats.

Frozen Fruit Bar

It's easier than you think to make your own healthy popsicles!

Ingredients

2 cups cut-up summer fruit (strawberries, raspberries, peaches, cantaloupe, watermelon, etc.)
1 tablespoon water
1 tablespoon sugar (optional)
1 teaspoon fresh lemon juice (optional)

Blend the fruit in a blender until smooth. Add a tablespoon of water to help make the consistency smooth. If you want, you can add a tablespoon of sugar for sweeter bars or a tablespoon of lemon juice for tarter flavor.

Pour the fruit blend into an ice-pop mold or paper cups. Insert sticks or a plastic spoon and freeze until solid. Enjoy!

Fruit Soda

$\frac{1}{2}$ cup fruit juice (Orange juice or an orange/pineapple juice combination works well.)

$\frac{1}{2}$ cup soda water or seltzer water

Fill a glass with $\frac{1}{2}$ cup of your favorite juice and $\frac{1}{2}$ cup of either seltzer or soda water. Stir and enjoy!

Name: _____ Date: _____

Calculate the Caffeine

Below is a list of a dozen drinks and snacks. They all have caffeine, but some pack a bigger punch than others. Work with a partner to put them in order from the most amount of caffeine to the least. All beverages are 12 ounces. Read the food labels or check the Internet to find the caffeine content.

2 NoDoz™ tablets	coffee	black tea	Mountain Dew™
1 cup coffee ice cream	Pepsi™	Diet Coke™	brownie
1.5 oz. dark chocolate bar	hot chocolate	7-Up™	Coke™
1.5 oz. milk chocolate bar			

Most Caffeine

1. _____

2. _____

3. _____

4. _____

5. _____

6. _____

7. _____

8. _____

9. _____

10. _____

11. _____

12. _____

13. _____

Least Caffeine

Name: _____ Date: _____

How Much?: A Caffeine Graph

Fill in the graph to show the different levels of caffeine for the drinks and snacks from the **Calculate the Caffeine** sheet. Remember to label your graph.

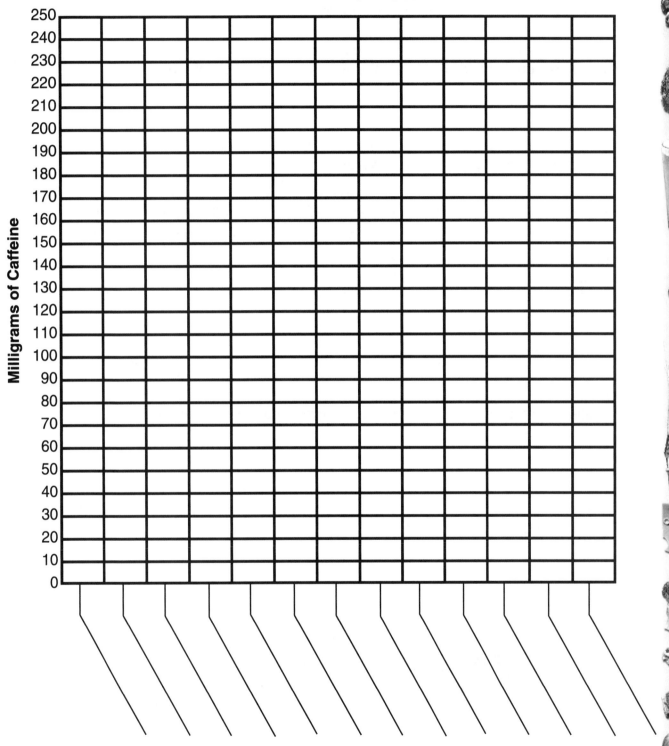

Drinks and Snacks

Name: _____ Date: _____

Caffeine 101

Like most people, you probably know someone who just can't start the day without a cup of coffee. They *need* that caffeine. Why do they feel that way? How does caffeine work? Test your knowledge by circling the correct answers in this caffeine quiz.

1. When we regularly drink or eat caffeine, it affects the chemistry of our brains.

　　T　　　　F

2. Circle all of the effects caffeine can have:

feeling happier　　　feeling more anxiety　　　feeling more energetic

feeling jittery　　　　feeling more alert　　　　feeling more sociable

unable to sleep　　　upset stomach

3. Caffeine can cause panic attacks.

　　T　　　　F

4. Caffeine can cause your heart to race and your muscles to twitch.

　　T　　　　F

5. If a person significantly cuts back on the amount of caffeine they consume, they can develop flu-like symptoms and might even start throwing up.

　　T　　　　F

Caffeine 101 Answers

Give yourself one point for each correct answer.

1. *True.* Caffeine actually affects our brain chemistry. As little as 30 mg of caffeine can have an impact on your brain chemistry and affect your mood and behavior. It only takes a few days of regularly consuming caffeine for our brain chemistry to start expecting the caffeine. Some people can become physically dependent and begin to experience withdrawal symptoms on as little as 100 mg of caffeine per day.

2. Give yourself 1 point for each of the following effects you circled.

   The positive effects: feeling happier, feeling more energetic, feeling more alert, feeling sociable. These positive effects are usually the result of lower levels of caffeine consumption.

   The negative effects: feeling anxious, feeling jittery, an upset stomach, and unable to sleep. These negative effects are often caused by high levels of caffeine.

   Different people have different tolerances for caffeine. How sensitive are you to caffeine?

3. *True.* Caffeine, particularly in higher doses, can cause panic attacks.

4. *True.* If you consume too much caffeine, your heart may start to race and your muscles may twitch. It can also cause tremors, anxiety, or restless and disconnected thoughts and speech.

5. *True.* When a person dramatically decreases the level of caffeine they consume, they can experience withdrawal symptoms, including:

headache	fatigue	sleepiness	difficulty concentrating
decreased motivation	irritability	depression	anxiety

   flu-like symptoms (nausea, vomiting, muscle aches, hot and cold spells)
   impairment in psychomotor and cognitive performance

   If you want to cut down on the amount of caffeine you consume, it's a good idea to decrease small amounts each day. This way, you are less likely to have these symptoms (and if you do, they are likely to be more mild). When you do cut down on caffeine, your brain chemistry adjusts quite quickly—in a matter of days—so the symptoms don't last long.

Scoring:
11–12:	You're ready for a Ph.D. Great job!
8–10:	You've been paying attention. Good work!
0–8:	You're on your way, but keep studying. Your body will thank you!

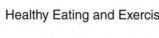

Finding a Healthy Weight: Fats, Friendly & Otherwise

Teacher Notes:

Fat is a health, taste, beauty, and more and more, a public policy issue. Cities are requiring labeling in restaurants and sometimes even banning trans fats. Millions of dollars are spent on diets and drastic surgeries to deal with unwanted body fat. What are the fat facts?

- New York City has banned trans fats, and Seattle is considering banning them. For **Law or No Law?** students create an ad arguing for or against a proposed law banning trans fats. Students may do research online about the trans-fat debate; alternatively, the class can talk through the pros and cons of banning the fats before they begin working on their ads.

- Healthcare providers use the **Body Mass Index** to determine if a person's weight is appropriate for their height. While there is a formula used to calculate this number, most healthcare providers use the chart included on page 50 to determine in which category a person falls. The exercise that goes with the chart is designed to help students grasp that even a modest weight gain or loss can lead to a big difference in a person's BMI and, thus, what category they fall into: underweight, normal, etc. Encourage students to realize that muscle weighs more than fat, so athletes might have obese BMI readings while having little body fat. Senior citizens and children should not use BMI readings because of differing bone mass densities. Other factors that can alter the accuracy of BMI readings include gender, race, age, and body type.

BMI	Category
15 or less	Starvation
15 - 18.5	Underweight
18.6 - 24.9	Normal
25.0 - 29.9	Overweight
30.0 - 39.9	Obese
40 or greater	Morbidly Obese

- For **What Do You Recommend?** students will need to consult the **Food Cards** from page 24. They can also use information from food packaging, manufacturers' websites, or the calorie counter at About.com (www.calorie-count.com), which lists products by food category.

- Students can use the fast-food menu on page 58 for **Fast-Food Trivia**, or they can print out menus from the websites of real fast-food restaurants that students visit.

Web Resources:

Students can play a game developed by the nonprofit Wellcome Trust designed to help them learn about the causes of obesity. In the game, they must raise a creature called an "ob" to age 20. The game can be found at http://www.wellcome.ac.uk/obs/activity.htm

Name: _____ Date: _____

Fats, Friendly & Otherwise

1. Fat in your diet is bad.

   T   F

2. Some cholesterol is good for you.

   T   F

3. If you have a high level of cholesterol, you are at greater risk of heart disease.

   T   F

4. Circle the foods that primarily have saturated fat:

butter	olive oil	canola oil	chicken with skin
steak	walnuts	whole milk	ice cream
fatty fish	avocados	peanuts	fast-food French fries

5. Circle the foods that primarily have unsaturated fat:

butter	olive oil	canola oil	chicken with skin
steak	walnuts	whole milk	ice cream
fatty fish	avocados	peanuts	fast-food French fries

6. Trans fats are the worst kinds of fat.

   T   F

7. To be considered **Low Fat**, a food should have _____ grams or less fat.

   a. 0   b. 2   c. 3   d. 10

8. When a food has _____ or more fat, it is considered **High Fat**.

   a. 5%   b. 10%   c. 20%   d. 50%

9. Circle the health conditions that are associated with obesity:

high blood pressure	asthma	diabetes	arthritis	back pain
high cholesterol	emphysema	sleep apnea	depression	

47

Fats, Friendly & Otherwise
Answers

Give yourself one point for each correct answer.

1. *False.* Fats are an important source of energy, are vital for proper growth and development, and are necessary for the absorption of vitamins A, D, E, and K. Fats also make food taste and even feel good in our mouths. The problem is when we have too much of a good thing.

2. *True.* Cholesterol is a fatty molecule that helps our bodies make estrogen and testosterone. It helps cells maintain their shape and nerves relay signals more efficiently. Our liver makes most cholesterol, but we still need to get approximately 300 mg from our food. Again, problems come with too much cholesterol, especially from animal sources.

3. *False.* Your total cholesterol is determined by the following formula: Total cholesterol = LDL + HDL + triglycerides/5. LDL is often called "bad" cholesterol; HDL is often called "good" cholesterol. Your total cholesterol may be high due to an elevated HDL, but this generally does not increase your risk of heart disease.

4. A saturated fat or oil often comes from animal sources, is solid at room temperature, and raises LDL cholesterol. The foods with primarily saturated fat are:

   butter   chicken with skin   steak   whole milk   ice cream   fast-food French fries.

   Give yourself 1 point for each saturated fat food you circled. Subtract 1 point for each unsaturated fat food you circled.

5. An unsaturated fat or oil often comes from plant sources, is liquid at room temperature, and lowers LDL cholesterol. The foods that primarily have unsaturated fat are:

   olive oil   canola oil   walnuts   fatty fish   avocados   peanuts.

   Give yourself 1 point for each unsaturated fat food you circled. Subtract 1 point for each saturated fat food you circled.

6. *True.* Trans fats are made when manufacturers add hydrogen to vegetable oils, making them partially hydrogenated. This causes a liquid oil to become a solid fat. These are the WORST fats to eat.

7. *c.* To be considered **Low Fat**, a food must have 3 grams or less fat.

8. *c.* When a food has 20% or more fat, it is considered **High Fat**.

9. Obesity increases the risk for all of these diseases. For an overweight person, even losing some weight will have significant impact on lowering their risk. Give yourself 1 point for each health condition you circled.

Scoring:
24–26:   You're ready for a Ph.D. Great job!
18–23:   You've been paying attention. Good work!
0–18:   You're on your way, but keep studying. Your body will thank you!

Name: _____ Date: _____

Law or No Law?

You work for an advertising agency that has been hired to create an ad campaign about a newly proposed law in your city. This law would ban the use of trans fats in all restaurants in the city as well as in any prepared foods sold inside the city limits. Should your ad be for or against this proposed law? Why or why not? Do some brainstorming, and then create your ad in the box below.

Reading the Body Mass Index Chart

BMI Number

Height (inches)	19	20	21	22	23	24	25	26	27	28	29	30	35	40
58	91	96	100	105	110	115	119	124	129	134	138	143	167	191
59	94	99	104	109	114	119	124	128	133	138	143	148	173	198
60	97	102	107	112	118	123	128	133	138	143	148	153	179	204
61	100	106	111	116	122	127	132	137	143	148	153	158	185	211
62	104	109	115	120	126	131	136	142	147	153	158	164	191	218
63	107	113	118	124	130	135	141	146	152	158	163	169	197	225
64	110	116	122	128	134	140	145	151	157	163	169	174	204	232
65	114	120	126	132	138	144	150	156	162	168	174	180	210	240
66	118	124	131	136	142	148	155	161	167	173	179	186	216	247
67	121	127	134	140	146	153	159	166	172	178	185	191	223	255
68	125	131	138	144	151	158	164	171	177	184	190	197	230	262
69	128	135	142	149	155	162	169	176	182	189	196	203	236	270
70	132	129	146	152	160	167	174	181	188	195	202	207	243	278
71	136	143	150	157	165	172	179	186	193	200	208	215	250	286
72	140	147	154	162	169	177	184	191	199	206	213	221	258	294
73	144	151	159	166	174	182	189	197	204	212	219	227	265	302
74	148	155	163	171	179	186	194	202	210	218	225	233	272	311
75	152	160	168	176	184	192	200	208	216	224	232	240	279	319
76	156	164	172	180	189	197	205	213	221	230	238	246	287	328

Weight (pounds)

Name: _____ Date: _____

Body Mass Index

What is Body Mass Index, or BMI? BMI is a simple numeric measure of a person's mass, based on weight and height. Medical professionals use BMI to determine whether or not a person is at a healthy weight. A doctor can figure out your body mass by multiplying your weight in pounds by 703, then dividing by your height in inches, and dividing by your height in inches again. You can also use the chart on page 50. Using the chart, figure out the BMI number for the people listed in the chart below.

Height	Weight (in pounds)	BMI Number
1. 5'2"	109	_____
2. 5'2"	120	_____
3. 5'2"	153	_____
4. 5'6"	124	_____
5. 5'6"	142	_____
6. 5'6"	186	_____
7. 5'10"	160	_____
8. 5'10"	181	_____
9. 5'10"	202	_____
10. 6'2"	171	_____
11. 6'2"	210	_____
12. 6'2"	272	_____

BMI is based on two numbers. Sometimes, it does not accurately reflect if a person is overweight or underweight. Can you think of some reasons why BMI would not apply to the following groups?

13. Athletes _____

14. Senior Citizens _____

15. Children _____

What are some other factors that could alter the accuracy of a BMI reading?

_____

_____

What Do You Recommend?

You are a health advisor with a client who wants to lose one pound this week. Review the client's food and exercise log for the previous week. What would you recommend to help your client reach his or her goal? Design an eating plan that includes whole grains, protein, and a fruit or vegetable with each meal. Keep in mind that snacks should include at least two of the following: protein, whole grain, fruit, or vegetable.

Reminder: People need to eat 3,500 fewer calories than they use in a week to lose one pound.

Last Week (All calories are in parentheses)

Monday:

Breakfast: a big bowl of Frosted Flakes™ with 2% milk (320) and an 8 oz. glass of Coke (97)

Snack: a Pop Tart™ (190)

Lunch: a hot dog (110), Cheetos™ (240), and an 8 oz. glass of Sprite™ (96)

Snack: 4 Oreos™ (100) and an 8 oz. glass of 2% milk (122)

Dinner: 6 chicken fingers (312), french fries (578), grapes (60), and 12 oz. of lemonade (135)

Exercise: none

Tuesday:

Breakfast: a granola bar (110) and 8 oz. of orange juice (110)

Snack: one chocolate donut (270)

Lunch: grilled cheese on white bread (320), Fritos™ (240), a banana (120), and a 12 oz. can of Pepsi (140)

Snack: a Fruit Roll-Up™ (80)

Dinner: a hamburger on a white bun (275), french fries (578), green beans (20), and a 12 oz. glass of 1% chocolate milk (160)

Exercise: none

Wednesday:

Breakfast: two pancakes and syrup (300) with a glass of whole milk (190)

Snack: one apple (80)

Lunch: turkey and cheddar cheese sandwich on sourdough bread (375), potato chips (220), and a 12 oz. can of Sprite (140)

Snack: a bowl of Goldfish™ (170)

Dinner: one pork chop (160), mashed potatoes (100), corn on the cob (65), and an 8 oz. glass of skim milk (90)

Exercise: 30 minutes of swimming

52

What Do You Recommend? (cont.)

Thursday:

Breakfast: an Egg McMuffin™ (300)
Snack: one banana (120)
Lunch: salad with crispy chicken and ranch dressing (270) and an iced tea with 2 tablespoons of sugar (50)
Snack: popcorn (110)
Dinner: macaroni and cheese (500) and water (0)
Exercise: none

Friday:

Breakfast: five french toast sticks (330)
Snack: one snack bag of pretzels (130)
Lunch: a ham and cheese sandwich on white bread (325), Cheetos™ (240), grapes (60), and 12 oz. of Powerade (120)
Snack: one Snickers™ bar (275)
Dinner: a hot dog (210), a bowl of strawberries and yogurt (210), and an 8 oz. glass of 2% milk (122)
Exercise: none

Saturday:

Breakfast: two whole grain waffles (180) and 8 oz. of orange juice (110)
Snack: whole grain crackers and a cheese slice (175)
Lunch: a hot dog (110), potato chips (220), and 16 oz. of Sprite™ (140)
Snack: one small bowl of Honey Nut Cheerios™ with skim milk (160)
Dinner: tacos with hard shells (370), corn on the cob (65), and water (0)
Exercise: an hour of moderate bike riding

Sunday:

Breakfast: none {overslept}
Snack: two Pop Tarts™ (380)
Lunch: a peanut butter and jelly sandwich (400), one snack bag of pretzels (130), grapes (60), and an 8 oz. glass of 2% milk (122)
Snack: one brownie (180) and an 8 oz. glass of 2% milk (122)
Dinner: one grilled chicken breast (140), a large salad with ranch dressing (125), one slice of sourdough bread (110), and water (0)
Exercise: None

Name: _____ Date: _____

What Do You Recommend? (cont.)

Write a food and exercise plan to help your client lose one pound this week.

Monday

Breakfast: _____

Snack: _____

Lunch: _____

Snack: _____

Dinner: _____

Exercise: _____

Tuesday

Breakfast: _____

Snack: _____

Lunch: _____

Snack: _____

Dinner: _____

Exercise: _____

Wednesday

Breakfast: _____

Snack: _____

Lunch: _____

Snack: _____

Dinner: _____

Exercise: _____

Thursday

Breakfast: _____

Snack: _____

Lunch: _____

Snack: _____

Dinner: _____

Exercise: _____

Friday

Breakfast: _____

Snack: _____

Lunch: _____

Snack: _____

Dinner: _____

Exercise: _____

Saturday

Breakfast: _____

Snack: _____

Lunch: _____

Snack: _____

Dinner: _____

Exercise: _____

Sunday

Breakfast: _____

Snack: _____

Lunch: _____

Snack: _____

Dinner: _____

Exercise: _____

Name: _____ Date: _____

Obesity in America: What Should We Do?

The Facts: Obesity in America is rising, even among children. As obesity rises, so do the serious health problems it causes.

The Question: Is this society's problem or an individual's problem? What, if anything, should we do? Ban fast food? Ban trans fats? Have P.E. every day in school? Should there be a public health information campaign? What are the costs for each approach?

Write a letter to the editor of a newspaper stating your opinion of how we should respond to the rising obesity rates in America.

Daily News

Monday Evening Edition   National News and Commentary   Sec. A

Dear Editor: Letters From Our Readers

Name: _____ Date: _____

Fast-Food Trivia!

Using your fast-food nutritional information sheets, create four **True-or-False** questions and four **Which-Has-More** questions. Can you stump your classmates? Be sure to include your answers, but don't let the other teams sneak a peek!

Examples: True or false: A large chocolate milkshake has more than 100% of your RDI (Recommended Daily Intake) for fat? Which has more calories, a Caesar salad with chicken or a hamburger and small fries?

True-or-False Questions:

1. _____

_____

Answer: _____

2. _____

_____

Answer: _____

3. _____

_____

Answer: _____

4. _____

_____

Answer: _____

Name: _____ Date: _____

Fast-Food Trivia! (cont.)

Which-Has-More Questions:

1. _____

   _____

   Answer: _____

2. _____

   _____

   Answer: _____

3. _____

   _____

   Answer: _____

4. _____

   _____

   Answer: _____

Name: _____ Date: _____

A Healthy Meal Is a Happy Meal

Use your fast-food knowledge to make smart selections. What's a healthy meal you would order from this menu?

Fast & Tasty's Fast Food Menu

ITEM	Calories	Sodium (mg.)	Saturated Fat (gm.)	ITEM	Calories	Sodium (mg.)	Saturated Fat (gm.)
Hamburger	250	520	3.5	Balsamic Vinaigrette Dressing	40	730	0
Cheeseburger	300	750	6	French Fries (small)	250	140	2.5
Double Cheeseburger	440	1150	11	French Fries (large)	570	330	6
Grilled Chicken Sandwich	420	1190	2	Chocolate Shake (small)	440	190	6
Crispy Chicken Sandwich	500	1130	3.5	Chocolate Shake (large)	770	330	11
Chicken Nuggets (six pieces)	250	670	3	Vanilla Shake with Candy Toppings	620	190	12
Chicken Nuggets (ten pieces)	420	1120	5	Milk	100	125	2.5
Chicken Ceasar Salad	220	890	6	Coca Cola™	110	5	0
Grilled Chicken Salad	300	890	1	Diet Coke™	0	15	0
Ranch Dressing	170	530	2.5	Powerade™	70	85	0

The Meal:

Total calories: _____   Total fat: _____   Total sodium: _____

Which food groups are represented in your meal? _____

_____

The healthiest thing about this meal is: _____

The Power of Protein: Meat, Beans, & Dairy

Teacher Notes:

Most Americans don't have a problem getting enough protein. The problem Americans face is that we get too much fat along with our protein. Most Americans could stand to eat more vegetables and beans. By introducing students to vegetarian options, you can show them how to include more vegetables and protein in their diets while reducing saturated fats.

- **Where's Your Protein From?** is designed to help students start to think about getting protein from a variety of sources, not just red meat. When your students have completed this page, you might want to ask them to share their answers and talk about what you find.

- Students will enjoy trying the **Homemade Yogurt** recipe in class. Higher fat milk helps the yogurt set more easily and reliably, but 2% works fairly consistently. 1% milk can work, but it is not as reliable, so we don't recommend it for beginning yogurt-makers!

- **What's a Vegan?** gives students some basic information about vegetarian eating habits. For this exercise, give students the top half of the page first, saving the answers for after they've completed the exercise. Students may not be aware that people do not eat animal products for religious or cultural reasons. There are a variety of books and cookbooks available to help students explore this topic in more detail.

- If you have access to vegetarian, Asian, or Italian cookbooks, you can easily extend **A Vegetarian Dinner** by having students plan a vegetarian menu of their own. You might even challenge them to come up with a week of vegetarian dinners!

Web Resources:

Learn more about heart-healthy seafood at: www.kidsafeseafood.org

The site www.thevegetarianchannel.com has links and resources about vegetarianism.

Name: _____ Date: _____

Where's Your Protein From?
A Protein Source List

Food	Grams of Protein
6 oz. hamburger	48.6
6 oz. chicken	42.5
6 oz. fish	41.2
1 cup cottage cheese	28.1
2 slices cheese pizza	15.4
8 oz. low fat yogurt	11.9
$\frac{1}{2}$ cup tofu	10.1
$\frac{1}{2}$ cup lentils	9
1 cup 1% milk	8
2 tablespoons peanut butter	8
1 oz. cheddar cheese	7.1
1 large egg	6.3
2 slices whole wheat bread	5.4
2 slices white bread	4.9
1 cup white rice, cooked	4.3
small baked potato	3
1 ear corn	2.6
1 cup of broccoli	2

Name: _____ Date: _____

Where's Your Protein From? (cont.)

Where is your protein coming from? Ideally, your protein should be coming from a variety of sources: meat, beans, dairy, and nuts, with small amounts from grains and vegetables. Did you eat enough protein yesterday? Where did it come from?

How much do you need?

Your weight _____ x 0.36 = _____ your daily protein needs (in grams)

How much did you eat yesterday?

Using the **Protein Source List,** write down all the protein foods you ate yesterday in the appropriate boxes, and then estimate how much of your daily protein you got. Did you get your protein from a variety of sources?

Beans	Dairy	Grains

Meat	Fish	Poultry

Eggs	Nuts & Seeds	Fruits & Vegetables

Satisfying Snacking

When you want a snack, it's easy to reach for junk food, but there are other options that are just as delicious and much better for you. Hummus, a popular dish from the Middle East, is a great choice.

Roasted Red Pepper Hummus

$\frac{1}{3}$ cup of sesame seeds

1 tablespoon olive oil

1 15 oz. can of garbanzo beans (also called chickpeas)

$\frac{1}{4}$ cup of lemon juice

2 garlic cloves

$\frac{3}{4}$ cup roasted red pepper

Toast the sesame seeds in a toaster oven for 5-10 minutes until golden. Cool for 15 minutes. Then blend them with the olive oil until smooth in a blender or food processor. Add the garbanzo beans, lemon juice, garlic cloves, and roasted red peppers. Continue blending until smooth.

Serve with pita bread, toasted pita bread, crackers, or fresh veggies like carrot sticks.

One of the great things about making hummus is you can play around with the ingredients. Don't like red peppers? Leave them out for a plain hummus. Want a different flavor? Add $\frac{1}{2}$ cup of fresh spinach or jalapeno peppers for a different dip every time.

Want a salty snack that's ready to go? Have a handful of nuts: they're rich in protein and vitamins.

Name: _____ Date: _____

What's Up With Moo?

1. We need calcium for:

    a. beautiful hair.   b. strong bones.   c. healthy teeth.   d. all of these.

2. More than 40% of children have gotten a cavity by the time they reach kindergarten; by the time students finish high school, nearly 80% have gotten at least one cavity.

    T   F

3. The only source of calcium in our diets is dairy products, like milk, yogurt, cheese, or ice cream.

    T   F

4. Dairy products, like milk, are hard for some people to digest.

    T   F

5. Most of your bone mass will accumulate before you reach the age of 20.

    T   F

6. Put these foods in order from most to least calcium:

    2 cups of broccoli   1 cup of nonfat milk
    1 cup of plain, nonfat yogurt   1 cup of tofu
    7 ounces of almonds   1 tablespoon of butter

    1. _____   4. _____

    2. _____   5. _____

    3. _____   6. _____

What's Up With Moo?
Answers

Give yourself one point for each question you answered correctly.

1. d. We need calcium for all of these things. Calcium is most important for our bones, including our teeth, but along with other vitamins and minerals, it helps our hair as well. Give yourself 3 points if you circled d., or 1 point for each item you circled.

2. True. More than 40% of children have gotten a cavity by the time they reach kindergarten; by the time students finish high school nearly 80% have gotten at least one cavity. Eating a calcium-rich diet, avoiding sodas, and brushing your teeth regularly can help limit your risk of cavities.

3. False. Dairy products, like milk, yogurt, cheese, or ice cream, are excellent sources of calcium, but they aren't the only ones. Leafy green vegetables, like spinach and broccoli, and some beans are good sources of calcium, as are cereals and drinks that are calcium-fortified.

4. True. Some people are lactose-intolerant, which means they have trouble digesting dairy products. Sometimes lactose-intolerant people can enjoy yogurt without any problems.

5. True. Most of your bone mass will accumulate before you reach the age of 20. That's why it is so important to get enough calcium while you are young!

6. Give yourself 1 point for each food you correctly placed in order from most to least calcium:

1. 1 cup of plain, nonfat yogurt
2. 1 cup of tofu
3. 1 cup of nonfat milk
4. 7 ounces of almonds
5. 2 cups of broccoli
6. 1 tablespoon of butter

Scoring:
11–13: You're ready for a Ph.D. Great job!
8–11: You've been paying attention. Good work!
0–8: You're on your way, but keep studying. Your body will thank you!

Homemade Yogurt

The yogurt at the grocery store often has a lot of added sweeteners and preservatives. Making your own yogurt is easy. You don't need any special equipment, just a stove, a pot with a good lid, and a warm spot. Once you've made plain yogurt, you can add your own fruit to custom make different flavors.

Ingredients

4 tablespoons of plain, low fat yogurt
6 cups of 2% or whole milk
fruit of your choice (optional)

Bring the milk just to a boil in a saucepan. Let it cool slightly, then add the yogurt. Mix well. Cover the pot and put it in an enclosed place, away from any drafts. The inside of an oven (make sure it is off!) is a perfect place. Yogurt needs a little warmth to set up properly, so turn the oven light on. If you put your yogurt in a cupboard, fill a glass jar with almost-boiling water and put it next to your pot. Leave the pot without opening it for 8 hours (overnight is perfect). When you open the pot, your yogurt should have set. Now you can add fruit and put your yogurt in the refrigerator. Remember to save some plain yogurt for your next batch!

What would you add?
Most people think of strawberries or cherries when they think of yogurt flavors. What would you add to your yogurt? Be creative!

Name: _____ Date: _____

What's a Vegan?

1. Circle which of the following reasons some people are vegetarians.

   a. don't like meat   b. religious reasons   c. environmental reasons
   d. healthy lifestyle   e. protecting animals   f. all of the above

2. A vegan will eat a grilled cheese sandwich.

   T   F

3. Circle the people who are/were vegetarians:

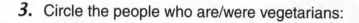

| Benjamin Franklin | Albert Einstein | Bob Dylan | Abraham Lincoln | Gandhi |
| Coretta Scott King | John Lennon | Henry Ford | Cesar Chavez | Hank Aaron |

4. A vegan will not wear leather, silk, or wool.

   T   F

- -

What's a Vegan? Answers

1. *f.* Some people are vegetarians for one or more of all these reasons. Religions that teach that eating meat is wrong include Hinduism, Jainism, and some forms of Buddhism. Give yourself 5 points if you circled f. or 1 point for each individual reason you circled.

2. *False.* A vegan will not eat a grilled cheese sandwich. Vegans do not eat any animal products, even if the animal was not killed in order to obtain that product. Regular vegetarians will eat a grilled cheese sandwich, as well as eggs and ice cream.

3. Everyone on this list except Abraham Lincoln was a vegetarian. Their reasons for being vegetarians were different. Some chose vegetarianism for health reasons. Others, like Gandhi and Cesar Chavez, were vegetarians for moral and ethical reasons. Give yourself 1 point for every person (except Lincoln) you circled.

4. *True.* Vegans not only do not eat any animal products, but they also don't use products made from animals in other ways either, including leather or fur.

Scoring:
   15–16:   You're ready for a Ph.D. Great job!
   10–15:   You've been paying attention. Good work!
   0–10:   You're on your way, but keep studying. Your body will thank you!

Name: _____ Date: _____

Mark the Menu

You are about to open a new restaurant. The menu is set, but a friend suggests that you mark the dishes that are vegetarian friendly. Put this symbol:  in front of the appetizers, salads, and entrees that a vegetarian can eat. Shade in the symbol if a vegan can eat the dish.

Appetizers

Garlic Bread: *French bread with garlic, butter, & spices* $3.50

Pita Bread: *Served with a side of yogurt & cucumber sauce* $3.50

Hummus: *Garbanzo beans, lemon juice, sesame paste, garlic, and pepper blended together and served with homemade pita bread* $4.50

Buffalo Wings $5.75

Salads

Caesar Salad: *Fresh romaine lettuce, lemon, parmesan cheese and croutons* $5.25

add Shrimp or Chicken $6.25

Greek Salad: *Tomatoes, cucumbers, green peppers, onions, olives, feta cheese, and house dressing* $5.95

Spinach Salad: *Baby spinach, tomatoes, red onions, walnuts, and goat cheese topped with raspberry vinaigrette* $6.50

Entrees

Spaghetti with Meatballs $8.50

Beef Ravioli $9.75

Cheese Stuffed Ravioli $9.25

Pesto Linguine: *Linguine noodles in an olive oil, garlic, and basil sauce* $8.50

Baked Meat Lasagna $9.50

Baked Veggie Lasagna $9.50

Mushroom Supreme Pizza: *Marinated mushrooms, homemade pizza sauce, and mozzarella cheese.* $10.00

4 Treat Special Pizza: *Pepperoni, Canadian bacon, sausage, and salami with homemade pizza sauce and mozzarella cheese.* $10.50

4 Cheese Pizza: *Swiss, parmesan, mozzarella, and feta cheeses* $10.00

A Vegetarian Dinner

You don't have to be a vegetarian to enjoy vegetarian dinners. Try this quiche and salad for a delicious taste of vegetarian-ism!

Quiche

Crust: 8 oz. low fat cream cheese
1 stick of butter
2 cups all purpose flour (for a healthier crust, use 1 cup of whole wheat with 1 cup of all purpose flour)

Filling: 4 new potatoes
1 cup chopped onion
$\frac{1}{2}$ cup diced red pepper
1 cup chopped asparagus
$\frac{1}{2}$ cup of shredded carrots
5 to 6 eggs
1 cup milk
1 tablespoon flour
1 cup grated cheddar cheese
salt and pepper to taste

Directions:
Cut the cream cheese and butter into the flour and roll it out. Gently lift into a pie pan, pressing it down gently as needed. Bake in 450° oven for 10 minutes. Cool for 5 minutes.

Cover the bottom of a frying pan in a very shallow layer of olive oil. Sauté the potatoes, onion, red pepper, asparagus, and carrots. When the potatoes are soft, scoop the mixture into the crust.

Meanwhile, mix the eggs, milk, salt, and pepper in a bowl. Separately, toss the cheese with the tablespoon of flour, and fold into the egg mixture. Pour this over the veggie mix in the pie pan. Bake for 1 hour at 350° or until the center is set. Cool for 15 minutes before serving.

Spinach Strawberry Salad

$\frac{1}{2}$ cup sugar
1 teaspoon olive oil
2 cups halved strawberries
6 cups torn spinach

2 tablespoons white wine vinegar
1 tablespoon chopped red onion
2 tablespoons slivered almonds

Combine the sugar, vinegar, olive oil, and onion in a clean, empty jar; cover tightly and shake. Toast the almonds under the oven broiler on low heat.
Combine the spinach and strawberries in a large bowl. Add the almonds and toss with the dressing immediately before serving.

68

Bringing It All Together

Teacher Notes:

There are many issues about our food supply today: Should genetically engineered crops be grown? Should they be regulated and labeled? Is organic food better for us and better for the planet? How can we keep our food supply safe? These are questions students will need to grapple with as consumers and citizens.

- Food allergies are rare, but they can be serious. Knowing what can cause an allergic reaction and how to treat it can help keep you and others around you safe. As with earlier activities, the answer sheet for **The 411 on Food Allergies** is designed to give students additional information.

- Students will need copies of **Bacteria: The Good, the Bad, & the Ugly** to complete the **Most Wanted: Bust These Bacteria** posters. When the students have completed their posters, consider cutting off the directions and posting their work in the school cafeteria, in nearby halls, or in bathrooms.

- The **Only Organic?** activity asks students to consider arguments for and against organic food and make up their own mind. Have students work in small groups and review the additional Web Resources or one of the many other websites about organic food. How did what they learned affect their opinions?

- For **You're the Buyer,** students will need access either to the Internet or a large collection of packaging and nutritional information. Assign each student or each small group of students a food category (cereal, snack foods/chips, cookies, canned fruits, canned vegetables, prepared soups, etc.) and have them decide what to stock within that category. Why did they make those choices?

- **Who Wants to Be a Healthy-ionaire?** will draw on all the things students have learned throughout their study of healthy eating and exercise. For **Who Wants to Be a Healthy-ionaire?** small groups of students will work together to create a list of questions and possible answers. They can use material in this book or outside sources to formulate their questions. When each group is ready, have them choose one person to be the questioner, and draw the name of a contestant from the rest of the class to play. As with the TV game, *Who Wants to Be a Millionaire*, allow contestants a set number of lifelines. This will be a great review for everyone.

Web Resources:

How Stuff Works: http://recipes.howstuffworks.com/organic-food.htm

USDA site on organic labeling: http://www.ams.usda.gov/nop/Consumers/brochure.html

Name: _____ Date: _____

The 411 on Food Allergies

1. Circle the 8 foods to which people are most commonly allergic:

   milk   eggs   wheat   sugar   soy

   peanuts   oats   shellfish   fish   salt

   tree nuts (like walnuts)   chocolate

2. You can have an allergic reaction to a food you have eaten before without any problem.

   T   F

3. People sometimes outgrow childhood food allergies.

   T   F

4. A runny nose, a skin rash, and tingling in the tongue can be signs of an allergic reaction.

   T   F

5. If someone eats peanut butter and their nose begins to run, they are definitely having an allergic reaction to the peanut butter.

   T   F

6. Wheezing, dizziness, abdominal pain, throwing up, and swelling in the throat can be symptoms of a food allergy.

   T   F

7. If you are severely allergic to a food, you can sometimes have a reaction from just touching it.

   T   F

8. "Food intolerance" is another name for food allergies.

   T   F

9. Sometimes it's OK to eat a really small amount of a food you are allergic to.

   T   F

10. There is medicine people can take if they are having a severe allergic reaction.

    T   F

11. Doctors can test for food allergies.

    T   F

12. If one of your parents has a food allergy, you are more likely to have a food allergy.

    T   F

13. People with food allergies should read food labels before eating a product.

    T   F

The 411 on Food Allergies Answers

Give yourself one point for each correct answer.

1. People are most commonly allergic to: *milk, eggs, wheat, soy, peanuts, tree nuts, shellfish, and fish.* Give yourself one point for each answer you correctly circled, but subtract one point for each wrong answer.

2. *True.* Some people develop allergies later in life.

3. *True.* People often outgrow childhood food allergies. However, some people never outgrow their allergies.

4. *True.* When a person has an allergic reaction, their immune system wrongly believes that a food is harmful. To protect the body, the immune system causes the body to release chemicals into the bloodstream called histamines. Histamines cause these symptoms.

5. *False.* There are many reasons a person might have a runny nose.

6. *True.* Other symptoms also include: hives, coughing, diarrhea, hoarseness, shortness of breath, heart racing, and decreased blood pressure.

7. *True.* Someone who is severely allergic may also have a reaction if they breathe tiny particles of the food in through their nose.

8. *False.* Although the symptoms of a food intolerance can be very similar to the symptoms of a food allergy, food intolerance is different from a food allergy. A food intolerance does not involve the immune system.

9. *False.* If you are allergic to a food, even a small amount of the food will trigger an allergic reaction. However, if you are just intolerant of that food, you may be able to eat a small amount without problems.

10. *True.* Severe allergic reactions can be treated with a shot of a chemical called epinephrine. People having a severe reaction should go to the emergency room immediately.

11. *True.* Doctors diagnose allergies by doing skin and blood tests, or by analyzing a patient's diet.

12. *True.* Food allergies can be hereditary.

13. *True.* Anyone with a food allergy should read the labels of all prepared or processed foods before they buy or eat them. Manufacturers are required to list if their product contains any allergenic foods in any form. They also must identify if the product was processed on machinery that also processed allergenic foods for other products. This helps people with allergies avoid having a reaction.

Scoring:
16–20:   You're ready for a Ph.D. Great job!
9–15:   You've been paying attention. Good work!
0–8:   You're on your way, but keep studying. Your body will thank you!

Bacteria: The Good, the Bad, and the Ugly

The Good

Bacteria is everywhere. Some bacteria help us digest food. Others are needed to make cheese, sour cream, and yogurt, among other foods. These bacteria are good for us.

The Bad and the Ugly

Other bacteria can cause food poisoning. The symptoms of food poisoning include: diarrhea, fever, chills, nausea, vomiting, and abdominal cramps.

Salmonella is a bad bacteria found in raw eggs, undercooked chicken or turkey, and improperly processed lunch meats. If you ingest the salmonella bacteria, symptoms usually start eight to 12 hours later. Most people will be sick for three to five days and usually do not require medical treatment. Avoid this bad bacteria by cooking your food thoroughly.

E. coli is spread by food or water contaminated with human or animal feces. E. coli can also be found in undercooked meats. Symptoms occur within eight days of ingestion and usually last three to four days. Treatment is needed only in the rare case of diarrhea lasting one week in adults or up to three weeks in children.

Campylobacter is found in undercooked chicken.

Botulism is rare and is usually found in home-canned food. Botulism has a different set of symptoms, which include double or blurred vision, droopy eye lids, slurred speech, difficulty swallowing, and muscle weakness. The symptoms start eight to 36 hours after ingestion. People with botulism poisoning need prompt medical treatment.

To Prevent Problems:

- Wash utensils, counter tops, and hands before and after you handle raw meat.
- Do not use food from dented or damaged cans.
- Use only pasteurized dairy products.
- Rinse fresh fruits and vegetables.
- Thaw frozen meats in the refrigerator before cooking.
- Heat foods thoroughly at the appropriate temperature.
- Refrigerate leftovers as soon as possible.
- Store fresh fruits and vegetables away from meat, poultry, and seafood.
- Disinfect cutting boards and sponges by running them through the dishwasher.

Call the doctor if:

- Your fever is over 101.5°.
- You have blood in your stool.
- You have prolonged vomiting that prevents you from keeping liquids down.
- You have signs of dehydration including decreased urination, dry mouth, and feeling dizzy when you stand up.
- You have diarrhea that lasts more than three days.

Name: _____ Date: _____

Most Wanted: Bust These Bacteria

Which of the bacteria from your **Bacteria: The Good, the Bad, & the Ugly** sheet do you think is the biggest public menace? Fill out the Most Wanted poster below with information about that bacteria.

MOST WANTED BACTERIA

WANTED FOR: _____

LAST SEEN: _____

ALIASES: _____

DESCRIPTION: _____

_____

CAUTION: _____

REWARD: _____

Name: _____ Date: _____

Only Organic?

What do you think are the two best arguments **for** growing, buying, and eating organic food?

1. _____

2. _____

What do you think are the two best arguments **against** growing, buying, and eating organic food?

1. _____

2. _____

Would you prefer to buy and eat organic food? Why or why not?

_____

_____

_____

_____

Do all the ingredients in a product have to be all organic in order for the product to be labeled

organic? _____

What do you think the rule should be? _____

_____

_____

Name: _____ Date: _____

You're the Buyer

You are the buyer for a small grocery store. You don't have a lot of shelf space, so you can only pick 10 brands or types of each product to stock in your product category, like soup, crackers, or canned vegetables. Consider both your need to make a profit and the desire to have a reputation as a store that sells healthy food. After researching the various brands in your product category, list the 10 brands/types of product you will choose to sell.

Product Category: _____

1. Brand/Type: _____

I picked this brand/type because _____.

2. Brand/Type: _____

I picked this brand/type because _____.

3. Brand/Type: _____

I picked this brand/type because _____.

4. Brand/Type: _____

I picked this brand/type because _____.

5. Brand/Type: _____

I picked this brand/type because _____.

6. Brand/Type: _____

I picked this brand/type because _____.

7. Brand/Type: _____

I picked this brand/type because _____.

8. Brand/Type: _____

I picked this brand/type because _____.

9. Brand/Type: _____

I picked this brand/type because _____.

10. Brand/Type: _____

I picked this brand/type because _____.

Name: _____ Date: _____

Who Wants to Be a Healthy-ionaire?

You've learned a lot about exercise and healthy eating. Now use what you've learned to write questions for a new game show called *Who Wants to Be a Healthy-ionaire?* Your questions should become harder as they are worth more money.

$100 Question: _____

_____

Answer choices:

  A: _____ C: _____

  B: _____ D: _____

$200 Question: _____

_____

Answer choices:

  A: _____ C: _____

  B: _____ D: _____

$300 Question: _____

_____

Answer choices:

  A: _____ C: _____

  B: _____ D: _____

$500 Question: _____

_____

Answer choices:

  A: _____ C: _____

  B: _____ D: _____

$1,000 Question: _____

_____

Answer choices:

  A: _____ C: _____

  B: _____ D: _____

     76

Name: _____   Date: _____

Who Wants to Be a Healthy-ionaire? (cont.)

$2,000 Question: _____

_____

Answer choices:

    A: _____   C: _____

    B: _____   D: _____

$4,000 Question: _____

_____

Answer choices:

    A: _____   C: _____

    B: _____   D: _____

$8,000 Question: _____

_____

Answer choices:

    A: _____   C: _____

    B: _____   D: _____

$16,000 Question: _____

_____

Answer choices:

    A: _____   C: _____

    B: _____   D: _____

$25,000 Question: _____

_____

Answer choices:

    A: _____   C: _____

    B: _____   D: _____

Who Wants to Be a Healthy-ionaire? (cont.)

$50,000 Question: _____

_____

Answer choices:

    A: _____   C: _____

    B: _____   D: _____

$100,000 Question: _____

_____

Answer choices:

    A: _____   C: _____

    B: _____   D: _____

$250,000 Question: _____

_____

Answer choices:

    A: _____   C: _____

    B: _____   D: _____

$500,000 Question: _____

_____

Answer choices:

    A: _____   C: _____

    B: _____   D: _____

$1,000,000 Question: _____

_____

Answer choices:

    A: _____   C: _____

    B: _____   D: _____